C000232889

THIS BOOK BELONGS TO...

Name: Age:

Favourite player:

2019/2020

My Predictions...	Actual...
The Foxes' final position:	
The Foxes' top scorer:	
Premier League Winners:	
Premier League top scorer:	
FA Cup Winners:	
EFL Cup Winners:	

Contributors: Peter Rogers

A TWOCAN PUBLICATION

©2019. Published by twocan under licence from Leicester City FC.

ISBN 978-1-911502-74-6

CONTENTS

Kasper SCHMEICHEL

01

POSITION: Goalkeeper   **COUNTRY:** Denmark   **DOB:** 5 November 1986

Whether it's been securing promotion to the Premier League or saving Champions League penalties, the Danish shot-stopper has proved he really is a top player during his time with the Foxes. Probably the first name on the team sheet each week, during the 2018/19 season he capped off another successful campaign with some fine saves against Chelsea on the final day.

THE 2019/20 SQUAD

James
JUSTIN
02

POSITION: Defender   **COUNTRY:** England   **DOB:** 23 February 1998

The former Luton Town full-back signed for Leicester City in the summer of 2019 and is an exciting young addition to the Foxes' defence. Following the departure of title-winner Danny Simpson, the English youngster will be eager to make his mark on the first team scene and will be working hard to challenge Ricardo Pereira for a starting place.

Ben
CHILWELL
03

POSITION: Defender   **COUNTRY:** England   **DOB:** 21 December 1996

Graduating from the Foxes' academy and growing into a mature defender, the England international has made the left-back shirt his own for club and country. Providing some fantastic assists for Leicester in the 2018/19 season, his sublime chip across the box to set up Demarai Gray's goal against Cardiff was just one of many highlights from an impressive campaign.

Çağlar
SÖYÜNCÜ
04

POSITION: Defender   **COUNTRY:** Turkey   **DOB:** 23 May 1996

A recent addition to the Foxes' defence, the young Turkish centre-back looked promising in his appearances during the 2018/19 campaign and is quickly adapting to life in the Premier League. With age on his side the youngster will certainly learn a lot from teammate Jonny Evans and club captain Wes Morgan as he looks to appear more for Leicester this season.

17

AYOZE
PÉREZ

THE LEGEND ROBERT HUTH

After initially joining the Foxes on loan in February 2015, Robert Huth played a vital role in the great escape in 2014/15. Huth headed home a dramatic and vital equaliser to bring Leicester level at 2-2 away to West Bromwich Albion in April. His goal came with ten minutes remaining and was the platform for Jamie Vardy's last-minute winner. That win at the Hawthorns was one of seven in the club's final nine games as Premier League survival was secured.

Always a man for the big occasion, Huth's goal against Tottenham in the 2015/16 Premier League title-winning season was certainly one to remember. After Harry Kane had missed a great chance to put Spurs 1-0 up at White Hart Lane, the German defender powered in a match-winning header to claim the three points for the visiting Foxes.

Upon arriving at Leicester on loan from Stoke the defender played a vital part in securing a much-needed point for the Foxes away at Everton in February 2015. As the Toffees pressed on the Foxes defence well into the second half, Huth made a vital challenge on John Stones to deny him a clear goalscoring chance.

On a huge occasion during Leicester's title-winning season, the Foxes hosted Chelsea at the King Power Stadium and both Huth, and manager Claudio Ranieri, faced their former club. As Huth kept the likes of Eden Hazard at bay for most of the game, the German helped the club to a historic 2-1 win.

In a must-win game during the 2015/16 season, the Foxes travelled to the Etihad to face Manchester City. Huth eased the nerves early on as he steered home a low cross in the first three minutes to open the scoring, before firing a rocket header into the top corner on the hour mark - Manchester City 1-3 Leicester.

9

CHRISTIAN FUCHS

2018/19

GOAL OF THE SEASON

Typically Christian Fuchs isn't known for his goalscoring prowess, however there's no doubt that the Austrian's superb strike against Fleetwood Town was rightly awarded Leicester City's 2018/19 Goal of the Season. In a game that the Foxes comfortably won 4-0 to progress to the next round of the Carabao Cup, the former Schalke 04 defender set the tone for the match as he opened the scoring in style in the eighth minute.

As Rachid Ghezzal's corner was sent in towards the six yard box the Fleetwood players comfortably headed the ball out of the penalty area towards Fuchs, who had only one thing in his mind as it bounced towards him. With his head down, the composed defender struck the ball cleanly with his left boot and the fans watched with bated breath as his 25-yard half-volley flew into the top corner. Opposition goalkeeper Paul Jones tried to get a hand to it, but he was certainly not at fault for conceding the goal. A game in which Ghezzal also netted a superb shot from a similar distance, Leicester eased past Joey Barton's side and demonstrated the gulf in class between the two teams.

Reminiscent of the goal he scored against Crystal Palace during the 2016/17 Premier League season, Fuchs' screamer against Fleetwood shone through as last year's Goal of the Season because of its sheer technical quality. A totally unstoppable hit, the Austrian's strike is yet another highlight to add to his career catalogue with the Foxes.

RUNNER-UP

RICARDO PEREIRA

The defender's winning strike against Manchester City was so close to being named 2018/19 goal of the season, however it just lost out to Fuchs' effort.

Picking up the ball on the edge of the box, Pereira smashed it home from a tight angle to earn the Foxes three points against the Premier League champions.

Wes
MORGAN

05

POSITION: Defender **COUNTRY:** Jamaica **DOB:** 21 January 1984

Playing with his heart on his sleeve, Wes has done just about everything with the Foxes since he joined the club in 2012 including captaining Leicester's Premier League-winning side in the 2015/16 season. The Jamaican defender chipped in with some goals at the tail end of the 2018/19 season, scoring in back-to-back games against Burnley and Bournemouth in March.

THE SQUAD 2019/20

Jonny
EVANS

06

POSITION: Defender **COUNTRY:** Northern Ireland **DOB:** 3 January 1988

A Premier League veteran appearing for Manchester United and West Brom for many a season, the central defender put in some fantastic performances for the Foxes in his debut campaign. A player who dominates the defensive area, his clearances and positioning show exactly how experience can boost a young side's confidence at the back.

Demarai GRAY 07

POSITION: Midfielder   **COUNTRY:** England   **DOB:** 28 June 1996

The young winger was signed from Birmingham City in 2016 and has been gradually adjusting his game to become a real attacking threat for the Foxes. As he continued to improve his scoring abilities throughout the 2018/19 season, Gray's opening goal against Cardiff will certainly be a memorable moment in the youngster's career.

Youri TIELEMANS 08

POSITION: Midfielder   **COUNTRY:** Belgium   **DOB:** 7 May 1997

The young central midfielder was loaned to the Foxes from Monaco in January and shined in his new surroundings with every performance. Already a fan favourite, Tielemans bosses the middle of the pitch with his two-footed passing and ability to push forward in attack. Linking up dangerously with Jamie Vardy, the pair are a handful for even the best Premier League defenders.

D Wears the Birmingham City captain's armband

Crystal Palace's nickname **E**

Danish Head Coach at Griffin Park

F

A Chelsea's Spanish skipper

B

Do you recognise this Championship club's crest

The Toffees play their home games here **G**

H Longest serving Championship manager and a Millwall legend

Followed Frank Lampard into the hot-seat at Derby County **C**

Foxes' Nigeria international signing who wears No.8

A-Z

2019/20 | PART 1

WHO'S WHO & WHAT'S WHAT OF ENGLISH FOOTBALL?

J Manchester City's Brazilian striker who was part of their 2019 Copa América winning side

K Polish international midfielder who was ever-present for Leeds United last season

L This England international has been with the Red Devils since the age of 7

M The Seagulls' Premier League top scorer last season

ANSWERS ON PAGE 62   15

AT THE TRAINING GROUND...

Come three o'clock on a Saturday afternoon, the fans get to see their heroes in action at the King Power Stadium.

Matchday is the day the Foxes' players, manager and coaching staff are all preparing for and focusing on throughout the week. All that preparation takes places at the club's training ground, well away from the watching eyes of the thousands of fans who flock to the King Power Stadium in hope of witnessing another winning performance.

The hard work begins in the summer months when the players all report back for pre-season training. The players are given a fitness programme to follow over the summer break and the first few days back at the training ground tend to involve a number of fitness tests. The results will enable Brendan Rodgers' coaching and fitness staff to assess each player's condition and level of fitness to ensure they are given the right workload over pre-season, so that they are fully match fit and raring to go for the big kick-off.

A lot of the work done over the pre-season period is designed to help the players reach a level of fitness that they can maintain for the entire campaign and perform at their maximum throughout the season.

When it comes to winning football matches, it is well known that practice, dedication and preparation are all vital ingredients for success. However, in terms of strength and fitness; rest, recovery and diet also play crucial parts in a footballer's welfare. The Leicester players are not only given the best of surfaces to practice on, but also given expert advice and guidance to ensure that they are fully equipped for the Premier League challenges ahead.

Technology also plays its part in helping the Leicester stars perform to their maximum. Prior to taking to the training pitches, players are provided with a GPS tracking system and heart rate analysis monitors ensuring that all they do, can be measured, monitored and reviewed.

And if all goes to plan, the team's drive, commitment and meticulous preparation on the training ground during the week, will pay dividends on matchday.

THE LEGEND DAVID NUGENT

After the Englishman arrived at Leicester in the summer of 2011, he was thrown into the Championship action straight away as the Foxes faced local rivals Coventry. In a game where City were victorious 1-0, Nugent was inches away from marking his debut with a goal as his close-range header struck the post.

When the former Portsmouth man did get his first goal for the Foxes it came during the side's 2-1 loss to Bristol City only a week after his August debut. Scoring in style for his new club, the recent signing buried a powerful strike from distance to level the scoreline.

As he continued to develop his game within his new surroundings, Nugent had an excellent season as Leicester earned promotion to the Premier League during the 2013/14 campaign. Scoring a whopping 20 goals, whilst developing a devastating partnership with fellow forward Jamie Vardy, the Foxes went all the way and won the Championship title.

One of the most magical games in Leicester's history came when the newly-promoted Foxes hosted familiar rivals Manchester United at the King Power Stadium in 2014. In the dramatic 5-3 victory, the ultimate comeback was particularly special for Nugent who scored his first Premier League goal with Leicester from the penalty spot.

Although the Foxes return to the Premier League was not welcomed with a comfortable season, Nugent provided a true highlight with his equalising strike against Liverpool in January 2015. Hitting his shot on the half-volley on the edge of the box, the Englishman bagged his second of the season and helped his side earn a point.

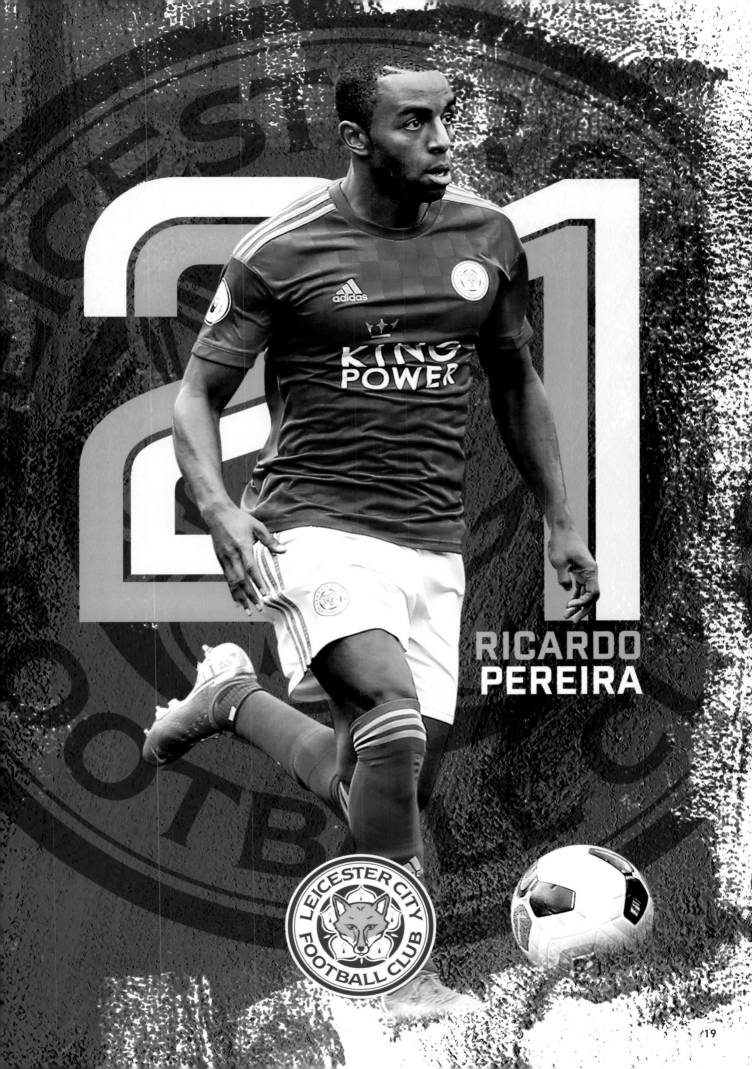

RICARDO
PEREIRA

LEICESTER CITY WOMEN

Since their establishment in 2004, Leicester City Women have rapidly grown into one of the most competitive sides in the Midlands. Playing their matches at the Farley Way Stadium since their move in 2017, the team has enjoyed a successful string of campaigns and are continuing to develop their squad in pursuit of FA Women's Super League football.

Having had their licence approved to join the FA Women's Championship - the tier just below the Super League - following restructuring of the upper divisions, LCWFC enjoyed a competitive 2018/19 season against some of England's strongest teams in both league and cup competitions.

As Jonathan Morgan's side kicked off the beginning of their Championship campaign with a 2-0 away victory over Crystal Palace, the Foxes set the tone for what would be a successful season in the second tier. Although hopes of a League Cup run were extinguished following defeats to Birmingham City and Sheffield United, the focus of the season seemed to be on league success; this was something certainly achieved following a string of positive results throughout September and October. With the likes of Melissa Johnson and Rosie Axten leading the scoring for the Foxes, Morgan's side were rarely goal-shy even when facing the toughest of competition.

Finishing the season solidly in seventh place at the end of the 2018/19 campaign, Morgan is aware of what the side needs to work on if they are to finish in a higher position in 2020. With the recent arrivals of former England Under-17 attacker, Lia Cataldo, and ex-Bristol City defender Grace Riglar, the club seems set on bolstering the squad at both ends of the pitch. With a talented, enthusiastic squad available at Morgan's disposal, it seems only a matter of time before the Foxes are challenging for the Championship top spots.

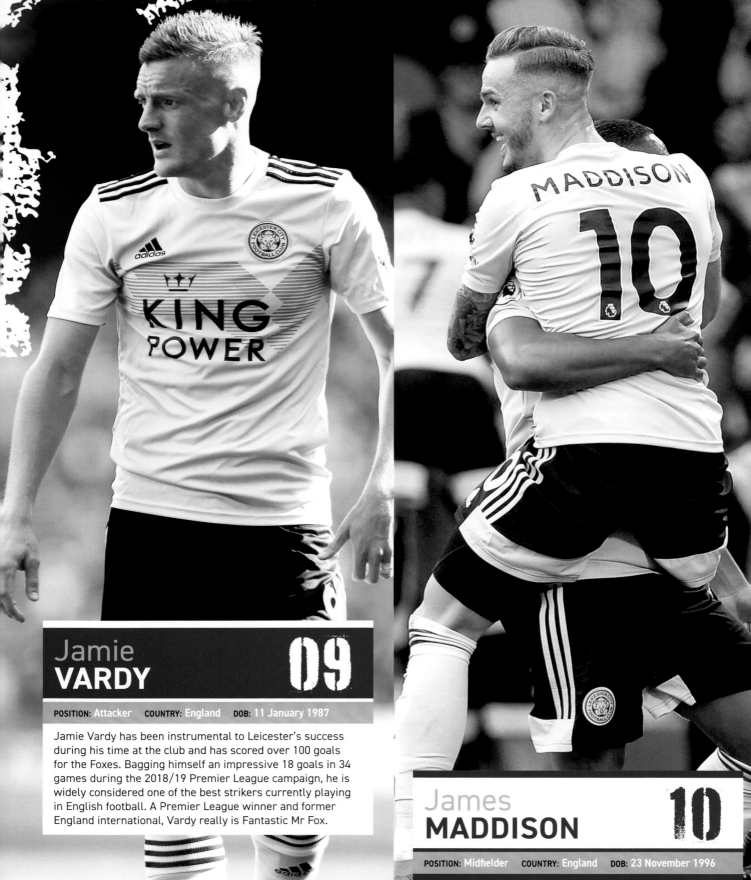

Jamie
VARDY
09

POSITION: Attacker **COUNTRY:** England **DOB:** 11 January 1987

Jamie Vardy has been instrumental to Leicester's success during his time at the club and has scored over 100 goals for the Foxes. Bagging himself an impressive 18 goals in 34 games during the 2018/19 Premier League campaign, he is widely considered one of the best strikers currently playing in English football. A Premier League winner and former England international, Vardy really is Fantastic Mr Fox.

James
MADDISON
10

POSITION: Midfielder **COUNTRY:** England **DOB:** 23 November 1996

The former Norwich City man has been excellent since his move to the King Power Stadium in the summer of 2018, scoring an impressive seven goals in his debut season in the Premier League. As well as showing slick feet and powerful free kicks, Maddison's ability to create space and opportunity for his team is nothing short of world class.

Marc
ALBRIGHTON
11

POSITION: Midfielder   **COUNTRY:** England   **DOB:** 18 November 1989

A confident wideman with a fantastic cross, Marc has remained at the heart of the Foxes squad since his arrival from Aston Villa in 2014. Scoring the dramatic equaliser against Manchester City in the 2018/19 season, the English midfielder also scored Leicester's first ever Champions League goal against Club Brugge during the 2016/17 campaign.

THE 2019/20
SQUAD

Danny
WARD
12

POSITION: Goalkeeper   **COUNTRY:** Wales   **DOB:** 22 June 1993

Although he wasn't a regular starter in the 2018/19 Premier League season, Ward became a fan favourite for his heroic penalty shoot-out saves against Wolves in the Carabao Cup. Making three epic stops to help seal Leicester's away win at Molineux, the 26-year-old has already demonstrated why he could be more involved for the Foxes in the next few years.

23

6

7

Can you figure out who these Foxes stars are?

8

WHO ARE YER

9

10

ANSWERS ON PAGE 62

25

WILFRED
NDIDI

Colour me!

15
HARVEY BARNES

Kelechi
IHEANACHO

14

POSITION: Attacker   **COUNTRY:** Nigeria   **DOB:** 3 October 1996

The former Manchester City striker has been a good addition to Leicester's attack since his arrival in 2017 offering both pace and height going forward. Typically paired with Jamie Vardy up front, Iheanacho scored a wonder-goal against Tottenham at the end of the 2017/18 Premier League season and showed exactly why he was nominated for the FIFA Golden Boy award in 2016.

Harvey
BARNES

15

POSITION: Midfielder   COUNTRY: England   DOB: 9 December 1997

A Leicester lad born and raised, Harvey Barnes really is "one of our own". Scoring his first Premier League goal against West Ham in front of the travelling Foxes fans in April 2019, the young attacking midfielder is an exciting prospect for both Leicester and England and has recently extended his contract with the club until 2024.

THE 2019/20
SQUAD

Filip
BENKOVIĆ

16

POSITION: Defender   COUNTRY: Croatia   DOB: 13 July 1997

Although he didn't appear for the Foxes during the 2018/19 season – having enjoyed an impressive campaign on loan with Celtic – the young defender is certainly an exciting defensive prospect. Towering over his opposition at six-foot and four inches, the former Dinamo Zagreb defender could prove to be a force to be reckoned with at both ends of the pitch.

29

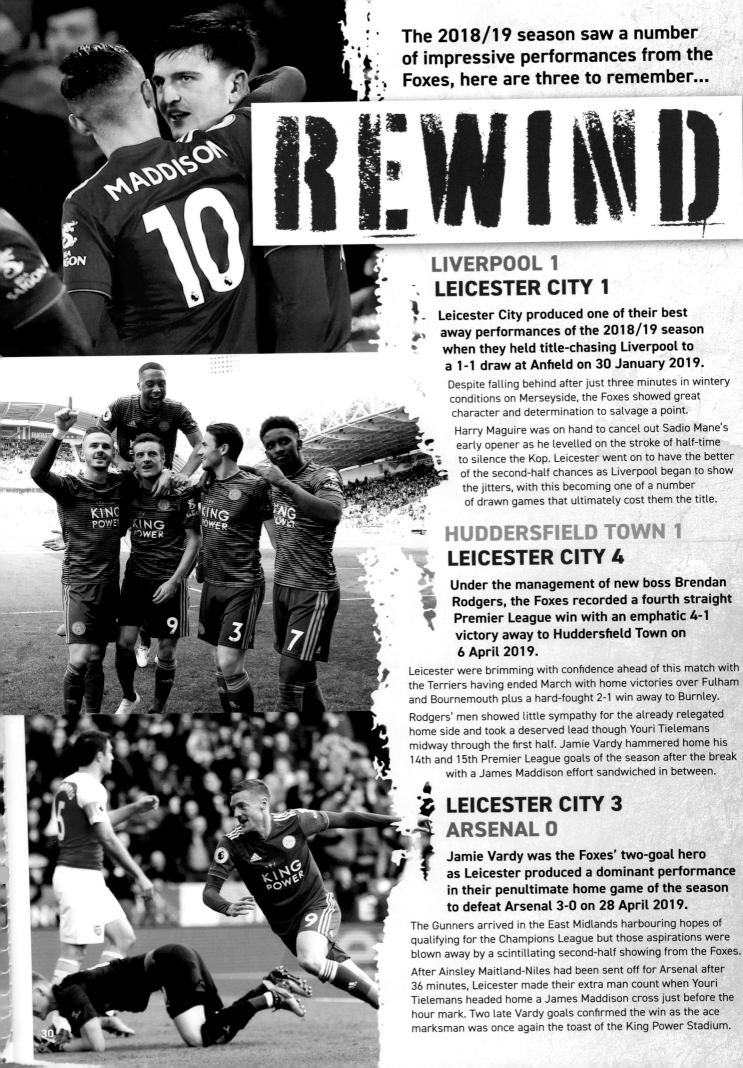

The 2018/19 season saw a number of impressive performances from the Foxes, here are three to remember...

REWIND

LIVERPOOL 1
LEICESTER CITY 1

Leicester City produced one of their best away performances of the 2018/19 season when they held title-chasing Liverpool to a 1-1 draw at Anfield on 30 January 2019.

Despite falling behind after just three minutes in wintery conditions on Merseyside, the Foxes showed great character and determination to salvage a point.

Harry Maguire was on hand to cancel out Sadio Mane's early opener as he levelled on the stroke of half-time to silence the Kop. Leicester went on to have the better of the second-half chances as Liverpool began to show the jitters, with this becoming one of a number of drawn games that ultimately cost them the title.

HUDDERSFIELD TOWN 1
LEICESTER CITY 4

Under the management of new boss Brendan Rodgers, the Foxes recorded a fourth straight Premier League win with an emphatic 4-1 victory away to Huddersfield Town on 6 April 2019.

Leicester were brimming with confidence ahead of this match with the Terriers having ended March with home victories over Fulham and Bournemouth plus a hard-fought 2-1 win away to Burnley.

Rodgers' men showed little sympathy for the already relegated home side and took a deserved lead though Youri Tielemans midway through the first half. Jamie Vardy hammered home his 14th and 15th Premier League goals of the season after the break with a James Maddison effort sandwiched in between.

LEICESTER CITY 3
ARSENAL 0

Jamie Vardy was the Foxes' two-goal hero as Leicester produced a dominant performance in their penultimate home game of the season to defeat Arsenal 3-0 on 28 April 2019.

The Gunners arrived in the East Midlands harbouring hopes of qualifying for the Champions League but those aspirations were blown away by a scintillating second-half showing from the Foxes.

After Ainsley Maitland-Niles had been sent off for Arsenal after 36 minutes, Leicester made their extra man count when Youri Tielemans headed home a James Maddison cross just before the hour mark. Two late Vardy goals confirmed the win as the ace marksman was once again the toast of the King Power Stadium.

Answer these questions on the 2018/19 campaign and see how much attention you were paying LAST SEASON!

1. Who made the most Premier League appearances for the Foxes last season?

ANSWER

2. Who put in the most Premier League tackles last season?

ANSWER

3. How many points did City finish the 2018/19 season with?

ANSWER

4. How many Premier League goals did the Foxes score last season?

ANSWER

5. What was the highest home attendance of 2018/19?

ANSWER

6. Against which club did the Foxes hit four goals last season?

ANSWER

7. Who won Premier League Player of the Month in April 2019?

ANSWER

8. Who knocked City out of the EFL Cup in the quarter-final?

ANSWER

9. Who received the most yellow cards in the Premier League last season?

ANSWER

10. Who came in on loan from Monaco in January 2019?

ANSWER

11. Who was the Foxes first signing of summer 2018?

ANSWER

12. Who top scored for the Foxes last season with 18 goals?

ANSWER

ANSWERS ON PAGE 62

FAST

FORWARD

There are lots of exciting games ahead for the Foxes in the second half of the 2019/20 Premier League campaign - here are three potential crackers...

MANCHESTER CITY (H)
22 February 2020

There is nothing like testing yourself against the best and 2018/19 Premier League champions Manchester City really were the best of the bunch last season.

The Foxes were one of very few teams that were able to get the better of Pep Guardiola's all-conquering side last term. Goals from Marc Albrighton and Ricardo Pereira gave Leicester a 2-1 win over City on Boxing Day 2018 but the visitors recovered to retain their Premier League title while also landing the Community Shield, League Cup and FA Cup in 2018/19.

City's clean sweep last season makes their visit to the King Power one of the most eagerly-awaited fixtures of 2019/20.

ASTON VILLA (H)
7 March 2020

After winning promotion via the end-of-season Play-Offs in May 2019, Midlands rivals Aston Villa are back in the Premier League for 2019/20.

The Villans are now the nearest top flight club to Leicester so there will certainly be a 'derby day' feel to their visit to the King Power Stadium on 7 March 2020.

The two sides produced a five-goal thriller as the Foxes mounted a memorable comeback the last time they faced Villa on home soil in September 2015. Trailing 2-0 with 18 minutes remaining, goals from Ritchie de Laet, Jamie Vardy and Nathan Dyer saw a grandstand finish as the Foxes won 3-2.

TOTTENHAM HOTSPUR (A)
9 May 2020

Unless the two clubs happen to face one another in a cup competition, the Foxes will make their first visit to Tottenham Hotspur's new stadium in May 2020.

Certainly a fixture that the travelling Leicester City fans will have been looking out for, the match at the 62,000-seater Tottenham Hotspur Stadium is the Foxes' final away game of the 2019/20 campaign and is sure to be worth the wait.

After almost two seasons playing their home games at Wembley, Spurs finally opened their new home in April 2019. The timing of Leicester's visit is sure to bring back memories of the crazy final game of 2017/18 when Spurs ran out 5-4 winners at Wembley.

32

PREMIER LEAGUE

PREDICTION FOR PREMIER LEAGUE WINNERS:

PREDICTION FOR PREMIER LEAGUE RUNNERS-UP:

CHAMPIONSHIP

PREDICTION FOR CHAMPIONSHIP WINNERS:

PREDICTION FOR CHAMPIONSHIP RUNNERS-UP:

THE FA CUP

PREDICTION FOR FA CUP WINNERS:

PREDICTION FOR FA CUP RUNNERS-UP:

EFL CUP

PREDICTION FOR EFL CUP WINNERS:

PREDICTION FOR EFL CUP RUNNERS-UP:

2020 PREDICTIONS

TEAMWORK

Every Premier League team is hidden in the grid, except one
Can you figure out which is missing?

Arsenal
Aston Villa
Bournemouth
Brighton and Hove Albion
Burnley
Chelsea
Crystal Palace
Everton
Leicester City
Liverpool
Manchester City
Manchester United
Newcastle United
Norwich City
Sheffield United
Southampton
Tottenham Hotspur
Watford
West Ham United
Wolverhampton Wanderers

```
J T S E W A K B M R R A T S T C B
E S O T E A S T O N V I L L A R Y
A Q E T S N N B H T E U F T E Y S
E B A O T A P R U V P B K Q O S D
V O J D H E S I M R D B I E V T N
I U T C A W N G E B N U C H I A Z
F R X E M R L H E Y F L K J M L P
M N J G U S I T A I Y O E A E P U
A E H O N R U O N M H X G Y P A S
O M B N I E S N F J H L N W L L A P
Y O D K T R Z A N J M O D Q R A P
T U E Z E E H N O H R E T A E C Y
I T T Y D D S D R K L E S S A E T
C H I U F N J H W I S B L S P C I
R N N D A A S O I W U E F P B U C
E F U H G W H V C A H M X D V B R
T E E I F N T E H C N F C G L Y E
S P L R F O E A C D C J I E T V T
E Y T N S T G L I V E R P O O L S
C W S O S P E B T R P G N Y F K E
I W A I V M D I Y V R I B E V H H
E Z C N D A K O E H X E M V I O C
L Q W E L H R N G O M O A E C H N
S M E J K R J S E W R N R R K U A
M A N C H E S T E R U N I T E D M
J A H G U V X B N N I G G O U T H
D I X A F L W M M Y A C L N V H C
C S D O J O L E K Y Z L T B Q S X
K Q B N T W A T F O R D W S Z I P
L F B Y U H N O T P M A H T U O S
```

34

ANSWERS ON PAGE 62

ÇAĞLAR
SÖYÜNCÜ

Q Ex-Hammer who made his debut for the Golden Boys last season

Middlesbrough keeper who played all 46 league games last season **R**

Joint Premier League top scorer last season alongside teammate Mané and Arsenal's Aubameyang

S

N France international who joined Spurs from Olympique Lyonnais in July 2019

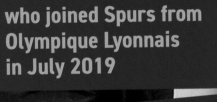

O

Goalkeeper and local lad who came through the ranks at Norwich

Nickname of Yorkshire club Barnsley **T**

U The Rams' team kit manufacturer

Former England international in the manager's seat at Craven Cottage **P**

The home of Championship new boys Charlton Athletic **V**

W Managed the Blades to promotion to the Premier League

LEICESTER CITY FOOTBALL CLUB

X Switzerland international who plays his home games at the Emirates Stadium

A 2019/20 PART 2

Z

WHO'S WHO & WHAT'S WHAT OF ENGLISH FOOTBALL?

Y The Magpies' international right-back with over 50 USA caps

Z Hammers defender capped over 50 times by Argentina

ANSWERS ON PAGE 62   37

AYOZE PÉREZ **17**

POSITION: Attacker   **COUNTRY:** Spain   **DOB:** 29 July 1993

After a very impressive second-half to his 2018/19 season at Newcastle, the Spaniard was a wanted man for a number of Premier League clubs in need of a proven goalscorer. Getting off the mark during Leicester's 2019/20 pre-season friendly against Scunthorpe, Pérez is quickly adapting to life with the Foxes and is already showing his true talent.

THE 2019/20 SQUAD

Daniel AMARTEY **18**

POSITION: Midfielder   **COUNTRY:** Ghana   **DOB:** 21 December 1994

A strong defensive midfielder who can also slot in at right-back, Amartey was unfortunate to have suffered a nasty ankle injury during Leicester's Premier League clash with West Ham in the 2018/19 season. Recently extending his contract at the club until 2022 however, the Ghanaian will be excited to step up to the next challenge now he has recovered.

Hamza
CHOUDHURY

20

POSITION: Midfielder   **COUNTRY:** England   **DOB:** 1 October 1997

After putting in a very good performance against Chelsea at Stamford Bridge during the 2018/19 season, Choudhury has begun to gain a lot of recognition for his dominant style of play and ability to regain possession of the ball. Having made a mark on the senior Leicester squad already, Choudhury also travelled to the UEFA Euro Under-21 tournament with England in the summer of 2019.

Ricardo
PEREIRA

21

POSITION: Defender   **COUNTRY:** Portugal   **DOB:** 6 October 1993

Thundering down the wing with electric pace and quick dribbling, the Portuguese defender is certainly unafraid of a challenge. After joining the club in the summer of 2018, the wideman adjusted to the Premier League quickly and dominated the right flank in just about every game he appeared in for the Foxes. Ruthless in both attack and defence, the Portuguese star has been a brilliant addition to the squad.

BURNLEY
TURF MOOR
CAPACITY: 22,546

MANCHESTER CITY
ETIHAD STADIUM
CAPACITY: 55,097

MANCHESTER UTD
OLD TRAFFORD
CAPACITY: 76,000

EVERTON
GOODISON PARK
CAPACITY: 39,572

LIVERPOOL
ANFIELD
CAPACITY: 54,074

LEICESTER CITY
KING POWER STADIUM
CAPACITY: 32,312

WOLVES
MOLINEUX STADIUM
CAPACITY: 31,700

ASTON VILLA
VILLA PARK
CAPACITY: 42,785

WATFORD
VICARAGE ROAD
CAPACITY: 21,577

SOUTHAMPTON
ST MARY'S STADIUM
CAPACITY: 32,384

BOURNEMOUTH
VITALITY STADIUM
CAPACITY: 11,329

NEWCASTLE UTD
ST JAMES' PARK
CAPACITY: 52,405

PREMIER LEAGUE GROUNDS 2019/20

Get a quick look at where the Foxes will be heading this season to take on their rivals.

Tick off the grounds once we've visited!

SHEFFIELD UTD
BRAMALL LANE
CAPACITY: 32,702

NORWICH CITY
CARROW ROAD
CAPACITY: 27,244

ARSENAL
EMIRATES STADIUM
CAPACITY: 60,260

TOTTENHAM HOTSPUR
TOTTENHAM HOTSPUR STADIUM
CAPACITY: 62,062

WEST HAM UTD
LONDON STADIUM
CAPACITY: 66,000

CRYSTAL PALACE
SELHURST PARK
CAPACITY: 25,456

CHELSEA
STAMFORD BRIDGE
CAPACITY: 41,631

BRIGHTON & HA
AMERICAN EXPRESS COMMUNITY STADIUM
CAPACITY: 30,666

41

YOURI
TIELEMANS

THE LEGEND
NEIL LENNON

As Leicester faced local rivals Coventry in August of the 1999/2000 season, Lennon picked up the ball outside the box and darted brilliantly through the defence before being fouled. As Muzzy Izzet slotted away the penalty to grab the only goal of the game, Lennon's tricky footwork earned the Foxes a famous win.

Although he didn't score dozens of goals for City, the Northern Irishman's strike against Southampton during the 1997/98 was truly magical. As Leicester chased an equaliser, Lennon got his head down and drilled his strike home from miles out to bring the scoreline level – the game ended Leicester 3 Southampton 3.

As Leicester pushed towards the 1998/99 League Cup final, their quarter-final clash with Blackburn was a real struggle for much of the game. A goalless deadlock until the 67th minute, Lennon placed a cheeky header into the bottom corner to help the Foxes progress dramatically into the semi-finals.

Following his contributions in the 1998/99 League Cup quarter-final, Lennon followed up his previous good work as Leicester faced Sunderland in the second leg of the semi-final. Fizzing in a perfect cross that was met by the boot of Tony Cottee, Lennon's assist cancelled out Niall Quinn's opener and sent Leicester to Wembley.

Although City didn't claim the League Cup in 1999, they won it the following year as they beat Tranmere Rovers 2-1 in the final. With Lennon appearing for the full 90 minutes, the midfielder lifted the trophy alongside captain Matt Elliott as Leicester became the last team to win the League Cup at the old Wembley.

Matty
JAMES

22

POSITION: Midfielder   **COUNTRY:** England   **DOB:** 22 July 1991

The former Manchester United player was signed by the Foxes in 2012 and has since remained a long-term figure in the Leicester City squad. James made most of his key appearances in the Championship however, with recent injuries stopping him from working his way back into the first team, his last Premier League appearance came during a 2-0 win over Brighton and Hove Albion in 2017.

Nampalys
MENDY

24

POSITION: Midfielder   **COUNTRY:** France   **DOB:** 23 June 1992

The defensive-minded Frenchman has been a solid addition to the squad since he arrived at the King Power Stadium in the summer of 2016. Representing France at various youth levels, the midfielder has great potential to play a holding role within the Leicester side - he was a regular starter under fellow Frenchman Claude Puel during the 2018/19 season.

Wilfred
NDIDI

25

POSITION: Midfielder   **COUNTRY:** Nigeria   **DOB:** 16 December 1996

Playing a powerful role in the middle of the park for Leicester, Ndidi continues to boss games and Premier League records each season. During the 2018/19 season he made a whopping 138 league tackles - the highest amount for any player at the end of that campaign - and showed why he has been named the Leicester City Young Player of the Season twice since arriving at the club in 2017.

THE 2019/20 SQUAD

THE LEGEND THEODOROS ZAGORAKIS

After completing a transfer to the Foxes in 1998 the former PAOK player marked his debut in style as Leicester comfortably beat Leeds United 1-0 in the Premier League. As Garry Parker's penalty bagged the points for City, the promising debut of Zagorakis was an indicator of what was soon to come.

Zagorakis' first goal for the club came in Leicester's 1-0 win over Barnsley during the 1997/98 season. Stealing the ball from the opposition on the half-way line and spreading it wide, the Leicester midfielder followed up the play and latched on to a low cross that had deflected in the penalty area before firing home.

Many fans will remember Zagorakis for his cameo appearance in goal for Leicester during their League Cup tie clash with Crystal Palace in the 1999/2000 season. After goalkeepers Pegguy Arphexad and Tim Flowers were withdrawn through injury, the Greece international went between the sticks and saw out a 3-3 draw for his side.

In a game that won't be cherished by Leicester fans for its scoreline – Leicester 2-6 Manchester United (1998/99) – Zagorakis provided a moment of genius to cancel out Dwight Yorke's opener. Picking up the ball outside the box, the midfielder skipped past the United players and blasted his effort past Peter Schmeichel into the top corner.

Despite only being with the Foxes for a brief spell, Zagorakis went to two League Cup finals with the club. Although he was an unused substitute in the second of the two, during Leicester's 1-0 loss to Tottenham the year before Zagorakis was a dominant force in midfield and was unlucky to not have claimed silverware that season.

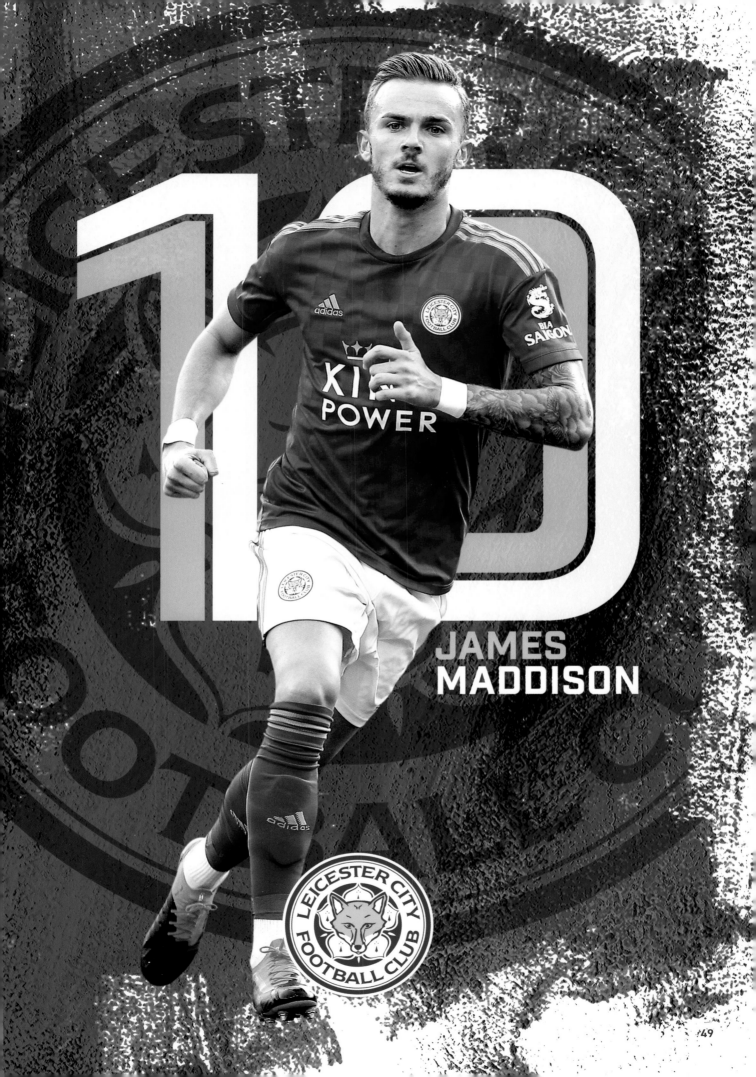

PREMIER
LEAGUE 2019/20

ARSENAL

ASTON VILLA

BOURNEMOUTH

BRIGHTON & HA

BURNLEY

CHELSEA

CRYSTAL PALACE

EVERTON

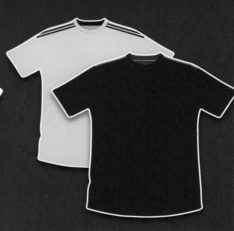

LEICESTER CITY

In a blue and white world, get to know your rivals in full Premier League colour!

LIVERPOOL

MANCHESTER CITY

MANCHESTER UNITED

NEWCASTLE UNITED

NORWICH CITY

SHEFFIELD UNITED

SOUTHAMPTON

TOTTENHAM HOTSPUR

WATFORD

WEST HAM UNITED

WOLVES

51

RICARDO
PEREIRA

2018/19

PLAYER OF THE SEASON

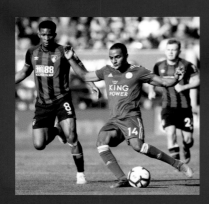

Signing from Porto in the summer of 2018, Ricardo Pereira looked an exciting prospect before he'd even played a game for the Foxes.

As the anticipation built for the 2018/19 campaign the Portuguese wideman didn't fail to deliver, quickly turning the hype into magical end-product. Providing a fantastic assist in his Premier League debut - helping Jamie Vardy net against a defensively-stubborn Manchester United - the defender then bagged himself two special goals against Everton and would-be champions, Manchester City.

As well as his attacking qualities shining through during his maiden campaign, it didn't take long before his defensive work was just as consistent. As he dominated the right flank and matched opposition players for pace and strength, Pereira showed exactly why fans were so excited about his arrival to the King Power Stadium. Having changed the look of Leicester's defence from the get-go, both Pereira and teammate Ben Chilwell began to demonstrate how vital the modern-day full-back can be to a team's success in the top division of English football.

Providing trickery in attack and a cool head in defence, Ricardo Pereira not only became 2018/19 Leicester City Player of the Season, but his efforts didn't remain unnoticed by his fellow players; earning him the Players' Player of the Season as well, it stands as a testament to his attitude and influence both on and off the pitch.

When considering that the 2018/19 season was his first in the Premier League, the 25-year-old couldn't have got off to a better start in his new surroundings.

YOUNG PLAYER OF THE SEASON

JAMES MADDISON

Showing great footballing intelligence throughout the 2018/19 campaign, James Maddison was rightly named the Foxes' Young Player of the Season in what was his first taste of top-flight, English football.

Scoring some fantastic free-kicks and bewildering opposition defences with his footwork, the former Norwich City man didn't look the least bit out of his depth alongside his fellow Foxes.

Stepping up at some vital moments to produce a piece of magic, his solo effort against Watford was particularly special and was a close contender for Goal of the Season. One of the most exciting English prospects in the modern game, it seems that James Maddison is only just getting started...

Dennis
PRAET

26

POSITION: Midfielder   **COUNTRY:** Belgium   **DOB:** 14 May 1994

Playing alongside compatriot Youri Tielemans at RSC Anderlecht, the two Belgian midfielders have been reunited at Leicester City after signing permanent deals in the summer of 2019. Having recently impressed during his time with Italian club, Sampdoria, Praet brings an exciting midfield flair to the Foxes' squad that looks to be a perfect addition to boss Brendan Rodgers' options.

Christian
FUCHS

28

POSITION: Defender   **COUNTRY:** Austria   **DOB:** 7 April 1986

One of the original Champions of 2015/16, Christian epitomises Leicester City's spirit and passion as a club. A real character on and off the pitch, the Austrian is a true professional and has committed himself to the club for many a season now. A decorated defender that the younger players look up to, Fuchs is a valuable part of the Foxes squad.

KING

Eldin
JAKUPOVIĆ

35

POSITION: Goalkeeper   COUNTRY: Switzerland   DOB: 2 October 1984

Since joining the Foxes in 2017, the experienced goalkeeper has stepped up to fill in for Kasper Schmeichel on a handful of occasions during his time with the club. Although he still has plenty of healthy competition for the starting shirt, Jakupović is an experienced player to have in the Leicester City squad.

THE 2019/20 SQUAD

JAMIE VARDY

Cover the wall
in posters!

Filbert Way

Leicester   LE2

The Foxes have boasted a wealth of talent over the years! Here is our...

FOXES DREAM TEAM

...see if you agree!

GOALKEEPER

1 SCHMEICHEL

KASPER SCHMEICHEL

One of the Premier League's most talented goalkeepers and part of the Foxes' 2015/16 title-winning team, Kasper Schmeichel was signed from Leeds United in 2011. A Danish international, he has played over 300 leagues games for Leicester.

YOUR CHOICE

RIGHT-BACK

2 WHITWORTH

STEVE WHITWORTH

A classy right-back, Steve Whitworth's performances for the Foxes saw him rewarded with seven England caps while at Filbert Street. A Second Division title winner in 1970/71, he made 353 league appearances for the club.

YOUR CHOICE

MIDFIELDER

6 LENNON

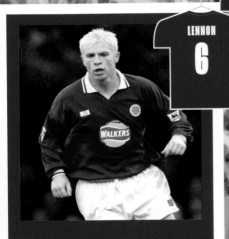

NEIL LENNON

Neil Lennon was Martin O'Neill's first signing as Leicester City manager, arriving from Crewe Alexandra in 1996. He was an inspirational figure as the Foxes won the League Cup in 1997 and 2000. He played 170 league games for Leicester City.

YOUR CHOICE

MIDFIELDER

7 DRINKWATER

DANNY DRINKWATER

All-action midfielder Danny Drinkwater was recruited from Manchester United in 2012 and went on to win the Championship title with Leicester City in 2013/14 and then became a Premier League champion with the Foxes two years later.

YOUR CHOICE

RIGHT WINGER

8 MAHREZ

RIYAD MAHREZ

Algerian winger Riyad Mahrez was a star performer in the Foxes' remarkable Premier League triumph in 2015/16. A true match winner, Mahrez was rewarded with the PFA Players' Player of the Year award in the title-winning season.

YOUR CHOICE

LEFT-BACK

CHILWELL
3

BEN CHILWELL

A member of the current Leicester City side who produces polished performances on a consistent basis in the Premier League. Ben Chilwell is a product of the Foxes' youth Academy and he made his full England debut at the King Power Stadium in a friendly against Switzerland.

YOUR CHOICE

CENTRAL DEFENDER

O'NEILL
4

JOHN O'NEILL

Northern Ireland international John O'Neill was capped 39 times while with the Foxes. He was a promotion winner with Leicester City in 1979/80 and again in 1982/83. A true club legend, he had a spell as captain and made 313 league appearances.

YOUR CHOICE

CENTRAL DEFENDER

ELLIOTT
5

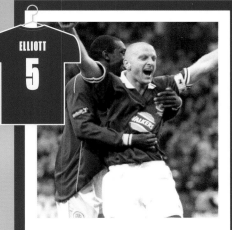

MATT ELLIOTT

A rock at the heart of the Foxes' defence, Matt Elliott was signed from Oxford United in January 1997 for a fee of £1.6M. A threat in set piece situations, he scored 26 goals in 243 league games plus a brace in the 2000 League Cup final triumph.

YOUR CHOICE

STRIKER

VARDY
9

JAMIE VARDY

The goalscoring sensation behind Leicester's never-to-be-forgotten Premier League title triumph in 2015/16, Vardy has been capped by England and remains one of the most feared strikers in the Premier League.

YOUR CHOICE

STRIKER

LINEKER
10

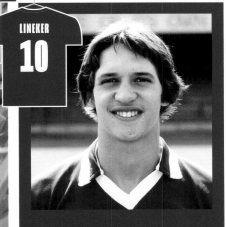

GARY LINEKER

Leicester-born Gary Lineker was the Foxes' top scorer in four consecutive seasons at Filbert Street. A star of the club's 1982/83 promotion success, Lineker scored an incredible 95 goals in 194 league games for the club.

YOUR CHOICE

LEFT WINGER

GLOVER
11

LEN GLOVER

Len Glover was a popular winger who featured in the Foxes' 1970/71 Second Division title-winning season. He arrived at Filbert Street in 1967 and starred in the Leicester side that reached the FA Cup final in 1969.

YOUR CHOICE

TOP 10

MOMENTS OF THIS YEAR

1.
2.
3.
4.
5.
6.
7.
8.
9.
10.

FOOTBALLERS OF ALL TIME

1.
2.
3.
4.
5.
6.
7.
8.
9.
10.

LEICESTER CITY MEMORIES

1.
2.
3.
4.
5.
6.
7.
8.
9.
10.

RESOLUTIONS FOR 2020

1.
2.
3.
4.
5.
6.
7.
8.
9.
10.

KASPER
SCHMEICHEL

1

KING
POWER

ANSWERS

PAGE 14 · A-Z PART ONE

A. César Azpilicueta. B. Bristol City.
C. Phillip Cocu. D. Harlee Dean.
E. The Eagles. F. Thomas Frank, Brentford.
G. Goodison Park. H. Neil Harris.
I. Kelechi Iheanacho. J. Gabriel Jesus.
K. Mateusz Klich. L. Jesse Lingard.
M. Glenn Murray.

PAGE 24 · WHO ARE YER?

1. Ben Chilwell. 2. Çağlar Söyüncü.
3. James Maddison. 4. Nampalys Mendy.
5. Wilfred Ndidi. 6. Ricardo Pereira.
7. Hamza Choudhury. 8. Jamie Vardy.
9. Ayoze Pérez. 10. Jonny Evans.

PAGE 31 · REWIND

1. Kasper Schmeichel, 38 appearances.
2. Wilfred Ndidi, 143 tackles.
3. 52 points. 4. 51 goals. 5. 32,149
(1 Sep 2018 v Liverpool, PL Round 4).
6. Huddersfield Town, 6 April 2019.
7. Jamie Vardy. 8. Manchester City.
9. Wilfred Ndidi, 8 yellow cards.
10. Youri Tielemans. 11. Jonny Evans.
12. Jamie Vardy.

PAGE 34 · TEAMWORK

Sheffield United.

PAGE 36 · A-Z PART TWO

N. Tanguy Ndombele. O. Aston Oxborough.
P. Scott Parker. Q. Domingos Quina.
R. Darren Randolph. S. Mo Salah.
T. The Tykes. U. Umbro. V. The Valley.
W. Chris Wilder. X. Granit Xhaka.
Y. DeAndre Yedlin. Z. Pablo Zabaleta.

PAGE 44 · HEY REF

1. Direct free kick. 2. Indirect free kick.
3. Yellow card - Caution.
4. Red card - Sending off. 5. Obstruction.
6. Substitution. 7. Offside/foul.
8. Penalty. 9. Offside location. 10. Play on.